T0389953

SilverTip

Our Moon

by D. R. Faust

Consultant: Jordan Stoleru, Science Educator

BEARPORT
PUBLISHING

Minneapolis, Minnesota

Credits

Cover and title page, © MelvinL/Adobe Stock; 3, © desertsolitaire/Adobe Stock; 4–5, © Ricardo Reitmeyer/Shutterstock; 7, © vladwel/Shutterstock; 9, © kinziramtane/Shutterstock; 11, © Claudio Caridi/Shutterstock; 12–13, © Iryna Rasko/Shutterstock; 17, © orin/Shutterstock; 18–19, © Public Domain/NASA; 20–21, © grayjay/Shutterstock; 23, © Claudio Caridi/Shutterstock; 25, © Shawshots/ Alamy Stock Photo; 26-27, © Public Domain/NASA; 28, © ttsz/iStock.

Bearport Publishing Company Product Development Team

Publisher: Jen Jenson; Director of Product Development: Spencer Brinker; Editorial Director: Allison Juda; Editor: Cole Nelson; Editor: Tiana Tran; Production Editor: Naomi Reich; Art Director: Kim Jones; Designer: Kayla Eggert; Designer: Steve Scheluchin; Production Specialist: Owen Hamlin

Statement on Usage of Generative Artificial Intelligence

Bearport Publishing remains committed to publishing high-quality nonfiction books. Therefore, we restrict the use of generative AI to ensure accuracy of all text and visual components pertaining to a book's subject. See BearportPublishing.com for details.

Library of Congress Cataloging-in-Publication Data

Names: Faust, D. R., author.
Title: Our moon / by D. R. Faust.
Description: Minneapolis, Minnesota : Bearport Publishing Company, [2026] |
   Series: Earth science—our planet: need to know | Includes
   bibliographical references and index.
Identifiers: LCCN 2025004594 (print) | LCCN 2025004595 (ebook) | ISBN
   9798895770696 (library binding) | ISBN 9798895775165 (paperback) | ISBN
   9798895771860 (ebook)
Subjects: LCSH: Moon—Juvenile literature.
Classification: LCC QB582 .F38 2026 (print) | LCC QB582 (ebook) | DDC
   523.3—dc23/eng/20250225
LC record available at https://lccn.loc.gov/2025004594
LC ebook record available at https://lccn.loc.gov/2025004595

For more information, write to Bearport Publishing, 3500 American Blvd W, Suite 150, Bloomington, MN 55431.

Contents

The Night Sky

What do you see when you look up at night? There might be twinkling stars. But most nights, the moon is the brightest object in the sky. That's because it is the closest object to Earth. What do you know about the moon?

The moon has long been a big part of life on Earth. It appears in many stories and songs from around the world. In the past, it was also used to track the seasons.

What Goes Around

A moon is a space object that travels around a planet. It goes in an **elliptical** path called an **orbit**.

Some planets have several moons. Others don't have any. Earth has one moon. Our moon travels around the planet about once every 27 days.

Moons are smaller than their planets. Earth's moon is about a quarter of the size of Earth. If our planet were a basketball, the moon would be the size of a tennis ball.

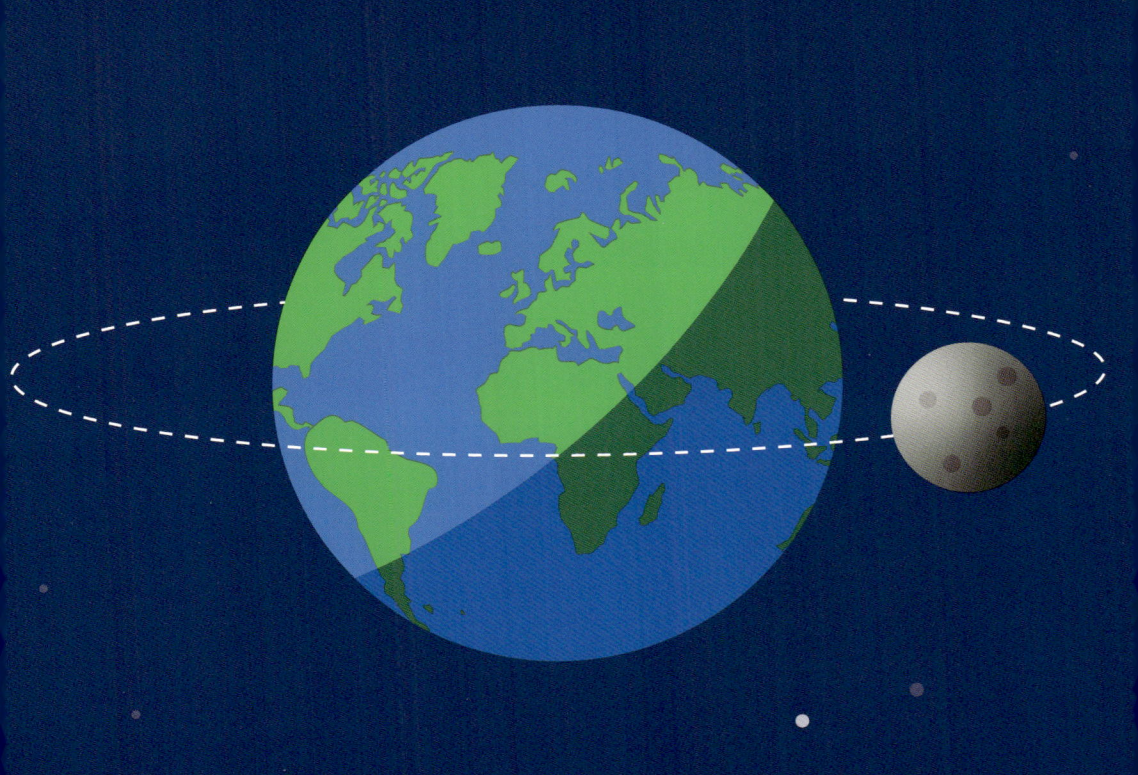

Tagging Along

What keeps the moon in its orbit? The answer is **gravity**. This invisible **force** draws objects together. Objects with more **mass** have a stronger pull than ones with less.

The sun's gravity keeps Earth in a path around the sun. And Earth's keeps the moon circling our planet.

Earth's gravity pulls things toward it. It is what keeps us on the ground. People have gravity, too. However, we have too little to affect Earth.

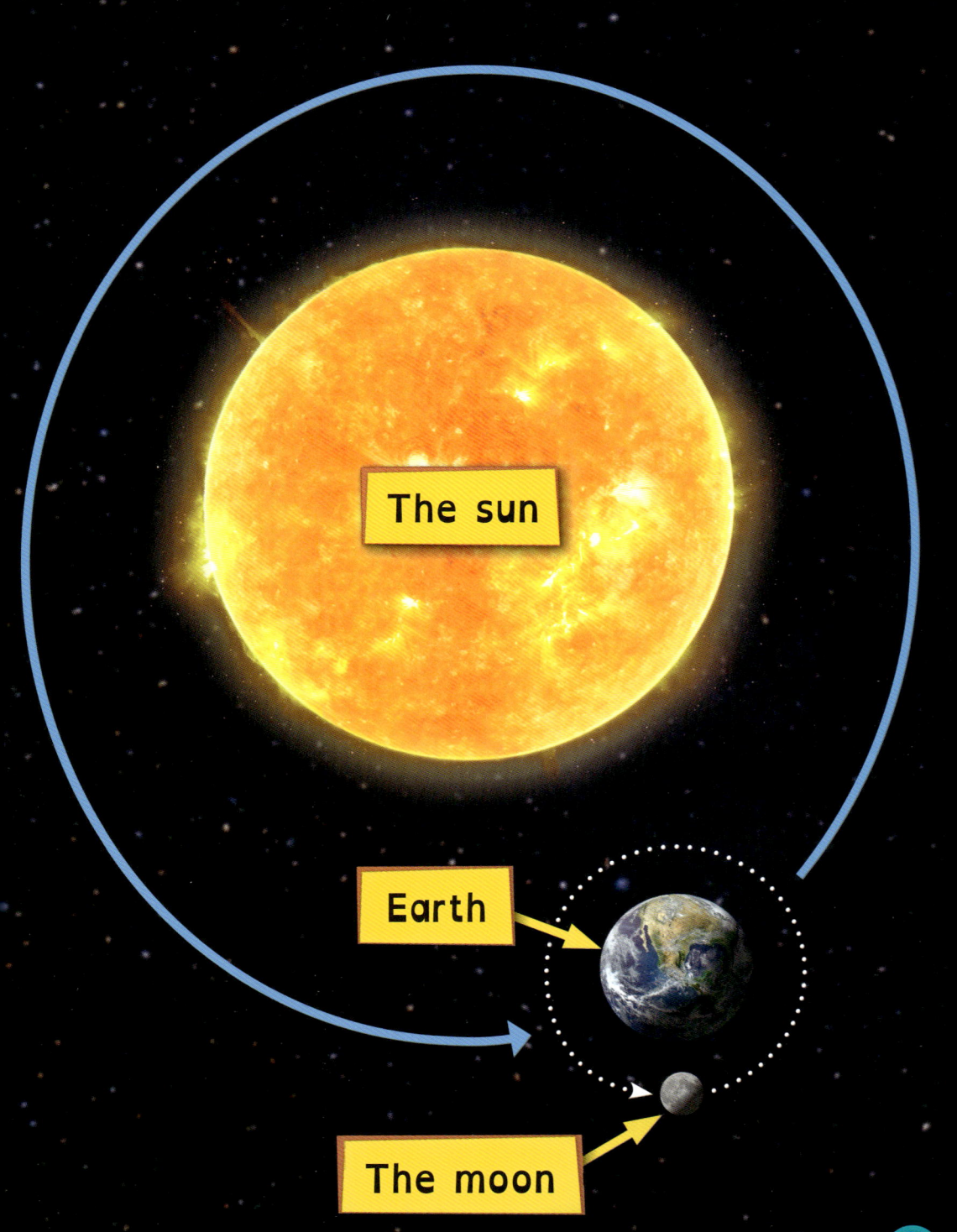

The sun

Earth

The moon

As the moon travels around Earth, both space objects spin. They rotate around imaginary lines. This line of rotation is called an **axis**.

Earth spins on its axis once every 24 hours. The moon makes only one spin every full orbit. This means the same side of the moon always faces Earth.

Early people broke time into months. These periods were based on about how long it took the moon to complete one trip around Earth. The word *month* even comes from the word *moon*.

Axis

11

Rising and Falling Tides

The moon's gravity is weaker than Earth's. However, it does still affect the movement of Earth's oceans. The levels of the ocean rise and fall in **tides**. The changing positions of Earth and the moon create these changes in water level.

Distance plays a part in how gravity works. The closer an object is, the stronger its pull of gravity. If you got close enough to the moon, its gravity would pull you in.

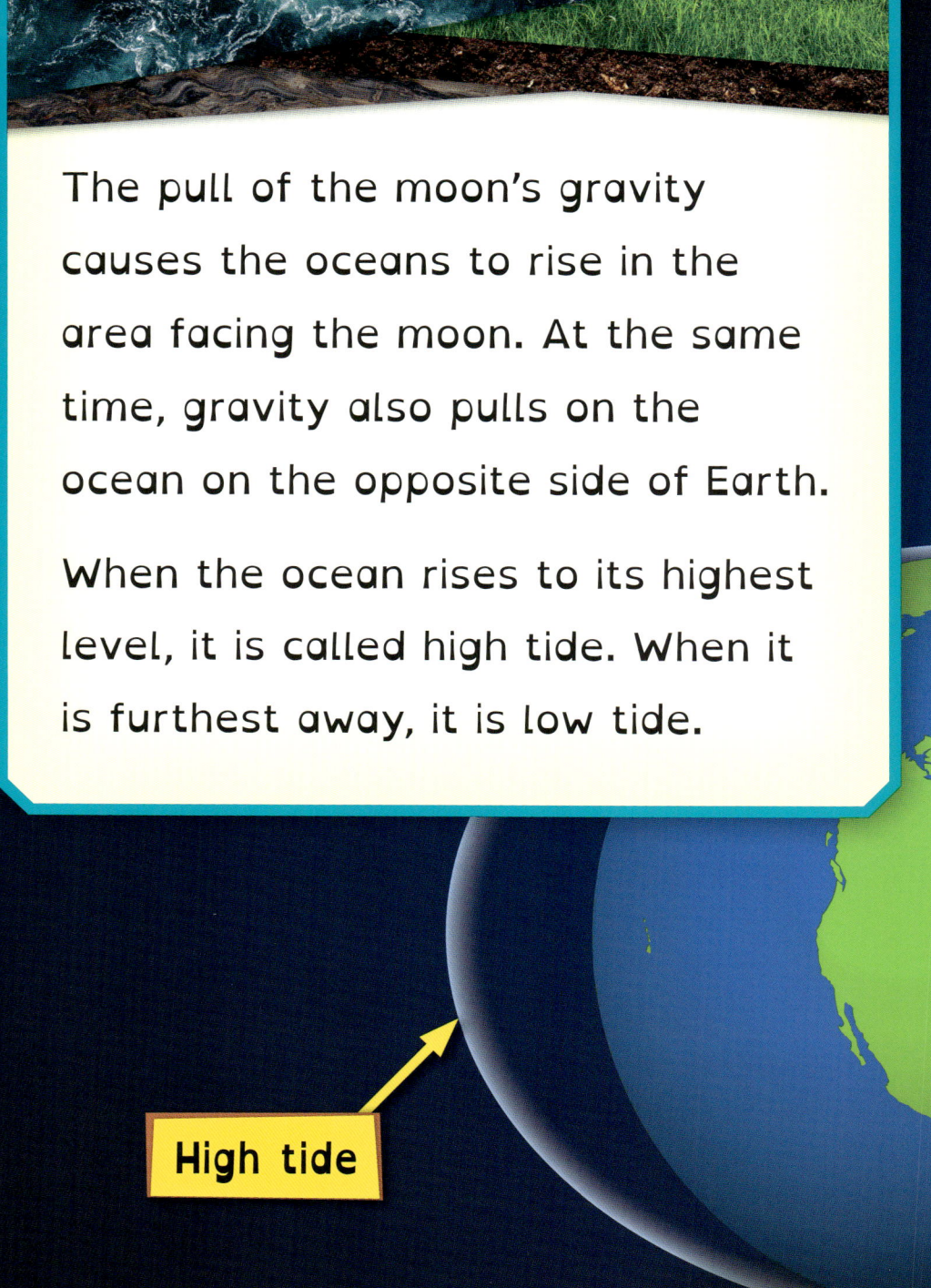

The pull of the moon's gravity causes the oceans to rise in the area facing the moon. At the same time, gravity also pulls on the ocean on the opposite side of Earth.

When the ocean rises to its highest level, it is called high tide. When it is furthest away, it is low tide.

High tide

Low tide

Most places along the coast have two high tides each day. One comes as Earth faces the moon. The other happens when the moon is on the opposite side of the planet. Low tides happen between the highs.

High tide

The moon

Low tide

Hit and Run

The moon is made of rock just like Earth. In fact, many scientists think the moon may have come from Earth. They believe Earth was hit by a large space object about five billion years ago. Huge chunks of Earth broke off. Gravity pulled the pieces together into the moon.

Some scientists think the moon formed another way. It may have come from somewhere else in the solar system. When it got close to Earth, gravity pulled it in. Then, the moon stayed in Earth's orbit.

Mountains and Craters

Like Earth, the surface of the moon is covered with rocks and dust shaped into **landforms**. The moon has many mountains. It has deep holes called **craters**. There are also large, flat areas called seas. These seas look like Earth's oceans, but they have no water.

Long ago, the moon had many volcanoes. These volcanoes are no longer active. However, they helped shape the moon's current landforms.

Changing Face

The moon seems to be lit up in the night sky. But it does not shine by itself. What we see is light from the sun reflected off the moon.

The part of the moon facing the sun is not always visible from Earth. This makes it look like the moon changes shape.

We are used to seeing the moon at night. However, sometimes the moon is bright enough to be seen during the day.

The changing shapes of the moon are called **phases**. They follow a regular cycle each month. When sunlight hits the side of the moon facing away from Earth, we cannot see it. As the moon orbits throughout the month, we see more and more. Eventually, the moon appears whole. Then, it shrinks back down.

It is called a new moon when we cannot see the moon at all. When we can see the whole thing, it is full. Halfway between new and full moons are quarter moons.

The main phases of the moon

New moon

First quarter

Full moon

Last quarter

One Small Step

The U.S. began planning a trip to the moon in 1961. Finally, on July 16, 1969, NASA launched the Apollo 11 spacecraft. Four days later, it reached its target. Neil Armstrong and Buzz Aldrin became the first people to walk on the moon.

Armstrong and Aldrin are not the only people to have visited the moon. Between 1969 and 1972, 10 other astronauts walked on the moon.

Buzz Aldrin on the moon

25

No one has stepped foot on the moon since 1972. However, several countries are currently planning missions there. Sending astronauts back to the moon may be a first step in more space travel. One day, we may send people to Mars . . . or beyond.

There are plans to build a base on the moon. It could be used for people to both live and work upon. People on the moon could test new space technology.

The Phases of the Moon

We see the phases of the moon based on how Earth, the moon, and the sun are positioned. The cycle takes about a month to complete. The images of the moon below show how it looks from Earth.

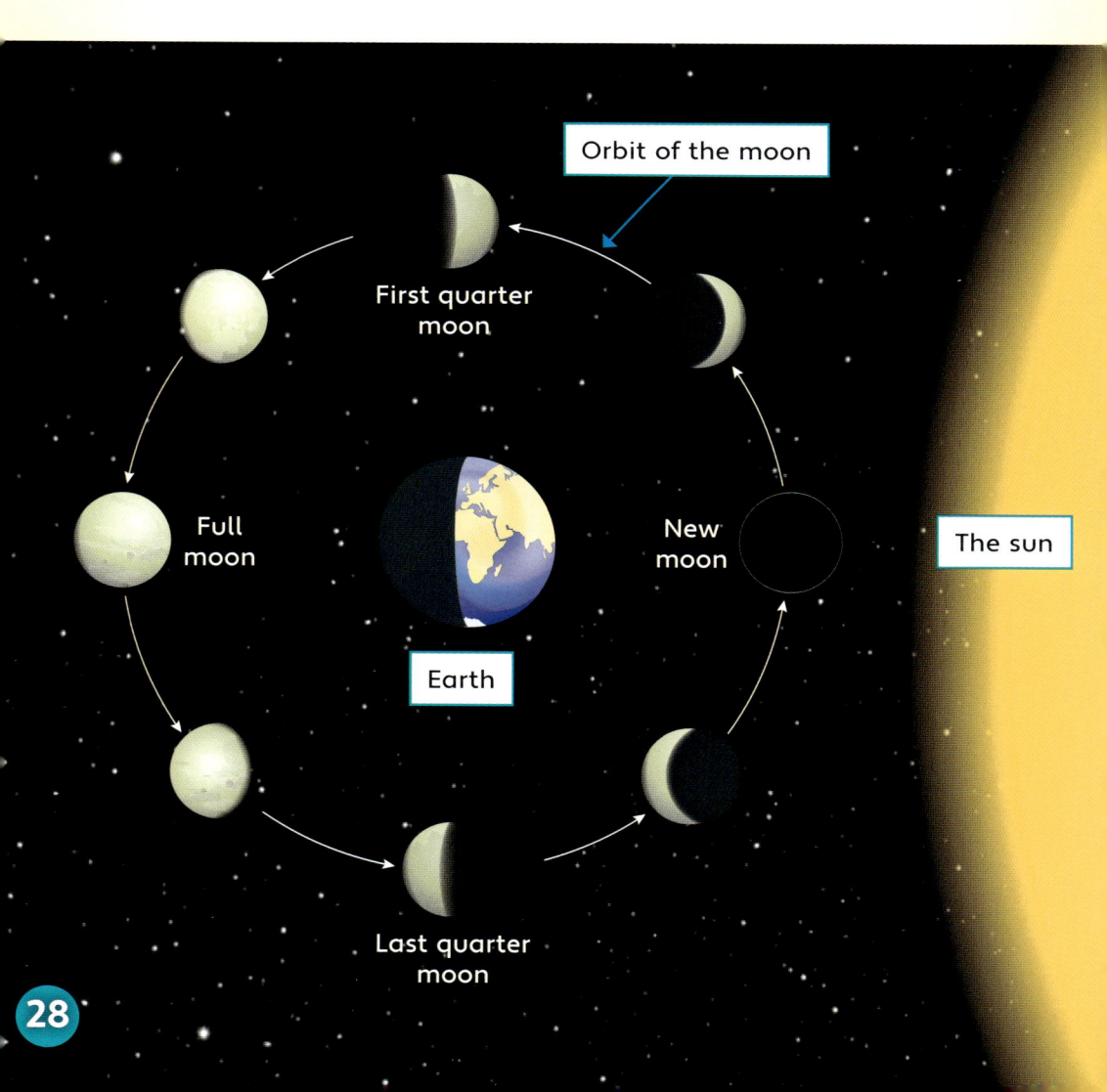

Orbit of the moon

First quarter moon

Full moon

New moon

The sun

Earth

Last quarter moon

★ SilverTips for REVIEW

Review what you've learned. Use the text to help you.

Define key terms

axis   phases
gravity   tides
orbit

Check for understanding

Explain what keeps the moon in orbit around Earth.

How does the moon affect life on Earth?

Why does the moon look different at different times of the month?

Think deeper

How would things be different on Earth if our planet did not have a moon?

★ SilverTips on TEST-TAKING

- **Make a study plan.** Ask your teacher what the test is going to cover. Then, set aside time to study a little bit every day.

- **Read all the questions carefully.** Be sure you know what is being asked.

- **Skip any questions** you don't know how to answer right away. Mark them and come back later if you have time.

Glossary

axis an imaginary line through a planet or moon, around which the object rotates

craters pits or holes made from rocks hitting a surface

elliptical oval-shaped

force a push or pull that can change the movement or shape of an object

gravity a force of attraction between all objects

landforms natural features on an object's surface

mass a measure of the amount or quantity of something

orbit the oval-shaped path of an object around a star, planet, or moon

phases steps or changes in a repeated series of events

tides the movement of water toward and away from shore

Read More

Adelman, Beth. *The Moon's Impact on Our Earth (The Moon Files).* Minneapolis: Lerner Publications, 2025.

Lilley, Matt. *The Moon (Amazing Space).* Mankato, MN: Creative Education, 2025.

Pierce, Simon. *The Artemis Program (Mission Control).* Buffalo, NY: PowerKids Press, 2025.

Learn More Online

1. Go to **FactSurfer.com** or scan the QR code below.

2. Enter "**Our Moon**" into the search box.

3. Click on the cover of this book to see a list of websites.

Index

About the Author

D. R. Faust is a freelance writer of fiction and nonfiction. They live in Queens, NY.